The Crab

Story by Jacquie Kilkenny
Photography by Lindsay Edwards

Robbie

Matt

Rigby®
A Harcourt Achieve Imprint

www.Rigby.com
1-800-531-5015

Matt and Robbie
ran down the beach
to the rock pools.

"I'm going to be the first
to find a crab," shouted Matt.

"No, I am," said Robbie.

The boys looked and looked
in the rock pools.

Mom walked up
to Matt and Robbie.

"Who can see some crabs?"
said Mom.

"I can see some seaweed
in here," said Robbie.

"I can see some shells,"
said Matt, "but no crabs!"

"It looks like it is going to rain," said Mom.

"We can't stay here for long."

Matt and Robbie went over
to a big rock pool.

"Here is a sea urchin,"
said Robbie. "Look at its spikes."

"But where are the crabs?"
said Matt.

"Matt! Robbie!" said Mom.

"We will have to go home now."

"Yes, Mom," said Matt.

"We are coming."

He looked at Robbie.

"Please help me find a crab."

The boys looked under the rocks.

"Here is a crab!"
said Matt.

"It was hiding under this little rock."

"You did find one!" said Robbie.

"Look at it go!"

"We are coming, Mom,"
shouted Matt and Robbie.